THE OUTGOING TIDE

BY BRUCE GRAHAM

DRAMATISTS
PLAY SERVICE
INC.

For B.J. Jones
and with thanks to Tim Evans and Candace Corr

THE OUTGOING TIDE was presented by the Delaware Theatre Company at 59E59 Theaters in New York City, opening on November 20, 2012. It was directed by Bud Martin; the assistant director was Larry McKenna; the set design was by Dirk Durossette; the costume design was by Wade Laboissonniere; the lighting design was by James Leitner; the sound design was by David O'Connor; the original music was by Patrick Lamborn; the stage manager was Marguerite Price; and the assistant stage manager was Caitlin Lyons. The cast was as follows:

GUNNER .... Peter Strauss
JACK .... Ian Lithgow
PEG .... Michael Learned

THE OUTGOING TIDE was presented by the Philadelphia Theatre Company (Sara Garonzik, Producing Artistic Director; Shira Beckerman, Managing Director) at the Suzanne Roberts Theatre in Philadelphia, opening on March 23, 2012. It was directed by James J. Christy; the set design was by David Gordon; the costume design was by Pamela Scofield; the lighting design was by R. Lee Kennedy; the sound design was by Bart Fassbender; the original music was by Robert Maggio; the production stage manager was Amanda Robbins-Butcher; the assistant stage manager was Danielle Commini; and the production dramaturg was Carrie Chapter. The cast was as follows:

GUNNER .... Richard Poe
JACK .... Anthony Lawton
PEG .... Robin Moseley

THE OUTGOING TIDE was originally commissioned as the recipient of the annual Selma Melvoin Playwriting Award, administered by Northlight Theatre, Chicago, Illinois. It opened at Northlight Theatre on May 22, 2011. The production was was directed by BJ Jones; the set design was by Brian Sidney Bembridge; the costume design was by Rachel Laritz; the lighting desgn was by JR Lederle, the sound design was by Andrew Hansen; and the production stage manager was Rita Vreeland. The cast was as follows:

GUNNER .... John Mahoney
JACK .... Thomas J. Cox
PEG .... Rondi Reed

CHARACTERS

GUNNER

JACK

PEG

PLACE

The Concannon home on the Chesapeake.

TIME

Autumn.

THE OUTGOING TIDE

ACT ONE

The Concannon home on the shore of the Chesapeake. It is not meant to be a totally realistic representation as it will turn into other things during the course of the play.

Different levels. The stage floor is the beach. The others represent a dock, a porch, and the inside of the home. Characters do not have to be held to reality with speaking to each other; they can speak while moving in and out of various areas and times.

This is a very rustic area. It faces west and gets great sunsets. It is autumn.

A light rises on Jack, 49. Nothing notable about him; a pleasant-looking man who — at the moment — seems a bit resigned to whatever might be happening in his life. He looks a bit out of place. His clothes and shoes are more suited to an office cubicle than beach walking.

At the edge of the beach stands Gunner. Gunner's in his early 70s but still a vibrant-looking guy. He wears the world's oldest, most comfortable fishing clothes and sits in an aluminum chair on the beach. His fishing rod sits in a holder next to a small cooler.

Although Jack is very polite, we get the feeling he'd rather be somewhere else at the moment. His conversation seems perfunctory most of the time, as if going through the motions.

GUNNER. See the nice part of bein' up this end of the bay is the water stays warm longer. You can still fish this time'a the year. You go about a mile south — to the canal there — forget about it. Too deep — too cold. Up here we got 'nother week or two. You fish?

JACK. No.

GUNNER. Don't buy your bait at Wal-Mart. Crap. Crawlers're dead half the time. Get your bait —

JACK. I don't fish.

GUNNER. — at the shack down the end of the marina.

JACK. I don't fish. *(A beat.)*

GUNNER. Then why the hell you wanta live here?

JACK. *(Shrugging.)* Well, I guess I —

GUNNER. Water. That's all ya got here. No nightclubs or anything.

JACK. I know … *(Jack picks up a couple of small stones to skip on the water. He will be silently disappointed with each throw.)*

GUNNER. Red Lobster. That's their idea of a restaurant 'round here. They don't even melt the butter right. Go figure. *(Watching Jack skip rocks.)* You're not too good at that, are you?

JACK. Guess not.

GUNNER. *(Grabbing a stone.)* My kid couldn't do it either. Spend half the summer out here practicin'. Think his record was two skips.

JACK. That so.

GUNNER. Got funny wrists, I guess. All inna wrist. *(Gunner skips one with ease. They both watch as it skims across the water.)* Five. Not bad. What kinda boat you got?

JACK. I don't have a —

GUNNER. No boat?

JACK. No, I —

GUNNER. Gonna get one?

JACK. Not planning on it. *(A beat.)*

GUNNER. You are gonna be really bored, my friend. Got kids?

JACK. Three.

GUNNER. They're gonna hate it here you don't have a boat.

JACK. They're —

GUNNER. But for God's sake don't get 'em a jet ski. They are the biggest pains in the ass. Wish I could find a piece'a piano wire 'bout a mile long — stretch it across at neck height. Settle their hash.

JACK. They're pretty much grown. All but the youngest — out of the house.

GUNNER. My kid hated it down here. Just our summer place

then. Couldn't wait to get home.

JACK. Really.

GUNNER. Hated to fish. Take that back. Didn't mind fishin'. He hated puttin' a crawler onna hook. It'd start ta wiggle, ya know, and he'd start ta cry. Baited his hook for him till he was like ten then I told him he was on his own. He's … not what you'd call "outdoorsy." He's a cook. Sorry, "chef." He's not gay though. Lotta those chefs're gay but he's not. Married. Owns a restaurant.

JACK. *(Suddenly interested.)* Really? A restaurant?

GUNNER. That's a tough racket. Thirty-eight percent of restaurants go outta business the first year, ya know.

JACK. That so?

GUNNER. Thirty-eight percent. *(Jack skips another stone — then reacts in pain, grabbing his neck.)*

JACK. Damnit …

GUNNER. You okay?

JACK. Got a … pinched nerve in my neck. Couple months ago. I keep thinking it's all better.

GUNNER. You need an ice pack?

JACK. No thanks —

GUNNER. Heating pad?

JACK. No, I —

GUNNER. Aspirin, ibuprofen, Ben-Gay, Aspercream? I'm old, I got everything in there.

JACK. I'm okay.

GUNNER. How'd you do that? *(A beat, as if Jack is reluctant to answer. Finally:)*

JACK. I … stood up.

GUNNER. Stood up?

JACK. I got up from the dinner table to take my plate to the sink and … it hit me. *(Gunner processes this.)*

GUNNER. Stood up. Okay … *(Gunner inspects his line. The bait has been stripped.)* Well, it's a nice bay here. I love tidal water. Makes ya think. Moon. Winds. Gotta take things into account. And with a tide you never know what you're gonna find onna beach. Every day, a little different. *(Pointing to the beach.)* All this dead stuff here. Leaves and everything. Tide tonight'll clean it right out. Never know it was here. *(Observing Jack.)* You a city guy?

JACK. Suburbs.

GUNNER. Well, you'll notice stuff down here ya never noticed before. Philly my whole life. Too many other things ta worry about. Don't pay attention, ya get hit by a bus. Down here, onna water — you start payin' attention to different stuff. *(Reaching for bait.)* It's nice ...

JACK. What're you using?

GUNNER. Pepperoni. Old pepperoni. Last New Year's or somethin'. Got hair on it.

JACK. They bite on that?

GUNNER. Catfish'll bite on anything. My buddy Salvy one time — he caught one onna sliver of soap. Unbelievable. Luckily I saw it 'cause Salvy was the biggest liar ya ever wanta meet. You like Jello?

JACK. Uhh ... sure. I guess.

GUNNER. Hate Jello. Never saw the point. *(He casts.)* Come on ... nice fat cat. *(The sound of geese comes from above. Both men look up for a moment, watching them.)*

JACK. Headin' south.

GUNNER. Rather them than me. Hate the south. You watch *Cops*? *(Although Jack answers, he's focussed on the geese.)*

JACK. Sometimes.

GUNNER. They gotta channel here shows it twenty-four hours a day. Almost always inna South. Man, those people're dumb. And they never wear shirts. Wanta get locked up? Go around without a shirt. *(The geese become louder as they watch.)*

JACK. That is so ... amazing. *(Off Gunner's look.)* The way they just get into that ... formation. Knowing where they're going. Knowing when to leave. *(The sound of the geese fades.)*

GUNNER. Lot smarter than a lotta people I know, that's for sure. Your wife like it here?

JACK. Uhhh, well — I'm sort of in the process of a divorce.

GUNNER. Sorry to hear it.

JACK. *(Avoiding.)* Well, you know ...

GUNNER. Readin' an article the other day about divorce. Some college in Denver did a study. Divorce rates out there and Tampa Bay, Miami and Phoenix all dropped. *(Very significant.)* After ... they got a Major League Baseball franchise. That is a fact. The minute they got baseball, people stayed married.

JACK. Really?

GUNNER. But these eggheads can't figure out why. I'm a high-school dropout and I got it clocked. Hundred and sixty-two games. On average say, four hours — with the pre- and post-game shows.

(Figuring quickly in his head.) That's 648 hours which — if you divide by twenty-four hours a day … *(Figures again.)* Comes to almost twenty-seven days. Twenty-seven days you can put on the TV or radio and ignore your wife. Common sense. My wife hates it here.

JACK.   Sorry to hear that. *(Unknown to them, Peg enters from around the house and stands above them. Late 60s but an energetic, good-looking woman who is dressed for gardening. Neither man notices her as she listens with interest.)*

GUNNER.   Used to love it when it was just a summer place but now we're here alla time — see, we always lived in Philly. Business there. Nothin' big — twenty-two trucks. Sold that, moved down here. Son lives out inna suburbs and all my friends — Jesus, old guys. They sit in McDonald's every morning for three hours drinkin' coffee and talkin' about their doctor's appointments. Why you gettin' divorced? *(Peg leans forward to listen.)*

JACK.   Oh … you know. Lotta things … I guess. Who knows?

GUNNER.   Which house is yours? *(Before Jack can react, Peg speaks up.)*

PEG.   This one. *(Surprised, they both look up to see her.)* That's Jack, Gunner. You're talking to Jack. *(She lets out a frustrated sigh and exits. The men stand in silence for a moment. Gunner looks confused, then regroups as Jack heads into the house.)*

GUNNER.   Who's that broad? *(Lights fade on Gunner.)*

PEG.   Now do you see what I mean?

JACK.   God, that was weird. We were talking — everything seems fine and then he … I mean, it took me a minute —

PEG.   I know.

JACK.   He starts telling me all this stuff I already know and I —

PEG.   It's happening so quickly.

JACK.   I see that —

PEG.   Worse, every day. Wait till he starts repeating himself. "Can we have pancakes tomorrow? Can we have pancakes tomorrow? Peg, tomorrow can we have pancakes? Peg, know what'd be good? Pancakes." And each time I tell him, "Yes, Gunner, we can have pancakes tomorrow," and five minutes later he's back about the pancakes and … and … the other day I — oh God, Jack, I snapped. I lost it. "Pancakes! I know, I know — you told me twenty … stinkin' times so far today!" *(She lets out a sigh.)* I felt … awful. The look on his face. It's not his fault. I have to keep telling myself that — it's not his fault. So I don't say anything. I just keep ... smiling and saying, "Sure, Gunner, we can have pancakes."

JACK. At first — when he started with the whole not knowing me thing — I thought he was pulling one of his bits —

PEG. "Bits?"

JACK. You know what I mean. I never know when he's telling the truth —

PEG. Oh, don't start this —

JACK. Come on, Mom — my whole life I never knew if he was lyin' to me or not. *(Lights rise on Gunner. We are in the past. When Jack speaks to his parents in these scenes he is — without overdoing it — a young boy.)*

GUNNER. Santa Claus is nothin' but a burglar, Jack. Don't believe that stuff they tell ya. He breaks into people's houses and steals toys.

JACK. But ... last year ...

GUNNER. I know. You got toys. But that's because I was waitin' for him. With a gun. See, if ya catch him then he leaves the toys he stole from somebody else. Go figure. Now, I'll be sittin' there this year too but just in case he gets past me ... hide your toys.

JACK. *(To Peg.)* You did it too, sometimes. *(Lights change on Peg. We are in the past with her now too.)*

PEG. You have to be very careful when eating fish, Jacky. I know a boy once who gulped down a piece of flounder, got a bone caught in his throat and he choked and died right there at the dinner table.

GUNNER. Those little chocolate eggs the Easter Bunny brings ya? Rabbit poop.

PEG. I know a boy who didn't look both ways and a big truck came around the corner and squashed him like a bug right in front of his house.

GUNNER. Watch it, Jack! Stay back!

JACK. Why, Dad?

GUNNER. Alligator!

JACK. *(Scurrying back.)* Where?

GUNNER. *(Pointing.)* Right there. I'll chase it away.

JACK. *(Terrified.)* Dad, don't!

GUNNER. Don't worry, son. I'll show 'em who's boss.

JACK. *(To Peg.)* So I just stood there. And I remember thinking how ... brave dad was. I was frozen ... horrified, as my father went out and wrestled ... a log. He won. *(He thinks a moment.)* I've never been comfortable swimming here.

PEG. I know a boy who sat too close to the television and his eyeballs melted and he fell over dead right there in the living room.

JACK. How did you know all those dead boys? *(As Jack speaks, lights change on Peg, back in the kitchen in present time.)*

PEG. I was just trying to teach by example.

JACK. Okay, fine. What's Dad's excuse?

PEG. He never lied, Jack. He just likes to tease. *(Puts a brochure in front of him.)* I want to show you something —

JACK. You showed me this a couple months ago —

PEG *(Plowing on.)* The place is beautiful. It is, Jack. My God, I felt so ... just ... good being there. Comfortable. Look at the brochure.

JACK. Mom, I don't have to —

PEG. Now you know I don't trust salespeople so I talked to some of the folks who lived there. And every one of them — a lot of them in the same boat with their husband or wife — love it. Love it. There is so much to do. Right in the middle of town. Busses run right past it and they have their own van that takes you places.

JACK. It's very nice.

PEG. You didn't even look at the brochure.

JACK. I —

PEG. Will you take a minute, please —

JACK. I was there.

PEG. You were?

JACK. Yes.

PEG. When?

JACK. Before I came down here.

PEG. Oh. Sorry, I didn't ... *(A whisper.)* Did you tell your father? *(An exaggerated whisper back.)*

JACK. He's outside.

PEG. He sneaks around now. He eavesdrops. If he could figure out the computer he'd read my email, I know it.

JACK. Well, the one part — the apartments and the gym and everything — was very nice.

PEG. And convenient.

JACK. You said.

PEG. It has a pool and a spa and —

JACK. I-was-there-Mom.

PEG. I'm sorry, I'm just … surprised.

JACK. You asked me to go a dozen times —

PEG. I was just surprised. And I'm not looking a gift horse in the mouth — I'm thrilled you came down for a visit, I was just —

JACK. Dad asked me.

PEG. Your father … he asked you to come down?

JACK. Called me the other night.

PEG. He asked you?

JACK. Yes. Of course he ended the conversation with, "Don't tell your mother," which is how most conversations end with you two. I wasn't going to tell you but now that I see how he is —

PEG. *(Ignoring him.)* Gunner called. Will wonders never cease. What did he say?

JACK. Just asked if I could come down.

PEG. That's all?

JACK. That's it.

PEG. *(A bit skeptical.)* Just … "come on down." No particular reason?

JACK. No.

PEG. Well, I'm glad you went to see it because I am going to need your help.

JACK. The part where you guys would live is great. Five-star hotel. It's … the hospital part — the A-Wing.

PEG. The personal care center.

JACK. Okay, whatever —

PEG. It's state of the art —

JACK. I'm sure it is.

PEG. Tim taught me that internet thing. I did research.

JACK. Okay.

PEG. You should really buy that boy some deodorant.

JACK. I've tried —

PEG. Last time I was there I snuck some of those air fresheners into his room.

JACK. I wish I hadn't seen the … A-Wing. Okay? My God, Mom, it's so depressing —

PEG. Oh, well pardon me, but it's filled with people who are dying. Maybe if they painted clown faces on them —

JACK. Okay, Dad … slips a little bit. He looks great —

PEG. He gets worse every day —

JACK. I can't picture him there. That's all. Okay?

14

PEG. I need help —

JACK. I know.

PEG. No, you don't. You haven't been here in months —

JACK. Two months, Mom. Not "months."

PEG. Two months is "months."

JACK. Yeah, but you're making it sound — forget it.

PEG. I need help here, Jack. He wandered away one night. I had to get in the car and — he was halfway to town. I lock the deadbolt at night and take the key. He doesn't know — don't tell him.

JACK. Jesus …

PEG. This cannot go on. Every day it's another battle over something … *(Lights rise on Gunner, who holds a remote.)*

GUNNER. TV's broke.

PEG. No, it's not.

GUNNER. I was tryin' ta —

PEG. *(Sighing.)* It's not broken.

GUNNER. Stop that. Hate that.

PEG. What?

GUNNER. The big sighhhhh. "The crazy old man's driving me nuts" sighhhhh.

PEG. The TV is fine.

GUNNER. Okay, I'm gonna go slowly here. It is plugged in. This is the right clicker. Not the one for the other things, the TV clicker. I have replaced the batteries in the clicker. I know they're good because they were still in the pack. Are you following me here? The batteries are in the right position — I double-checked. I point the clicker at the television — I push "power" — and nothing happens. Therefore, Peg, the goddamned TV is broken.

PEG. Gunner … that's the microwave. *(Lights fade on Gunner, rise on Jack.)* It's a hundred little things a day, Jack. You'll see. One minute he doesn't know who I am, the next he's telling me about an Easter dinner forty years ago. Half the time he talks to me he thinks I'm Salvy. I thought I was finally rid of Salvy. And some of the things he says … just … *(Silence.)* I am exhausted, Jack. And it's not as if he moves right into the … personal care center. We'll have one of the apartments and then … when he gets … bad — whatever — he moves over. It's not like I won't be there — I'll be there every day. Did they tell you about the classes?

JACK. No. What classes?

PEG. How to deal with him. How to feed him. Bathe him. Change

15

him.

JACK. Whoa, whoa, whoa — gimme a break.

PEG. What?

JACK. I do not want to talk about this.

PEG. You've changed diapers.

JACK. Not on my father!

PEG. No one's asking you to —

JACK. But just the ... image. Okay? Mom. The whole ... picture.

PEG. You think I like this? But we have to face some facts here —

JACK. *(Pointing outside.)* Aren't you kind of rushing things here? He's out there fishing. Perfectly fine and you've got him ... *(His voice trails off. She waits.)*

PEG. What? I've got him what?

JACK. Look, I'm just — not now, okay?

PEG. When?

JACK. I've been on the phone with my lawyer all morning —

PEG. There's a waiting list, Jack. If we want to get in on it, we have to make a decision. As in now.

JACK. What did he say about it? *(No reaction.)* Come on, Mom ... *(Lights rise on Gunner. A warm glow. Soft music plays in the background. We are in the assisted living facility.)*

PEG. You know your father.

GUNNER. Let's get the hell outta here.

PEG. If we got the two-bedroom —

GUNNER. You know how much they want for this place?

PEG. — then you could have a TV room of your own.

GUNNER. Jesus, lookit that old guy.

PEG. The pool's this way.

GUNNER. Building's on fire, don't get stuck behind him onna way out.

PEG. It's Olympic-sized.

GUNNER. All bent over. Looks like he got his tie caught in his zipper.

PEG. Do you want to see the pool or not?

GUNNER. When did you ever see me swim in a pool?

PEG. We never had a pool.

GUNNER. People pee in 'em. 'Course with this gang you're hopin' that's all they do.

PEG. Oh, and you're just perfect, aren't you? They're all a bunch of ... I-don't-know-what, but not you. Everything's fine.

GUNNER. Well, I don't have a basket and horn on my walker like that broad —

PEG. You almost burnt the house down. Should I announce that to everybody?

GUNNER. *(Angry, spinning on her.)* Jesus Christ —

PEG. Thank God for the smoke alarm —

GUNNER. Will you shut your goddamn mouth? *(Peg reacts — shocked. Gunner tries to reel it in.)* How many times I gotta apologize, huh, Peg? Crazy old man almost burnt down the house — you don't think that embarrasses the livin' hell outta me? I asked you nice a dozen times not to ever — *(In frustration he slaps the side of his head.)* I'm sorry — Jesus, I'm ... I can't stand talkin' to you like that but for God's sake, Peg — give it a rest, will ya? I'm sorry I put the damned ... paper on the stove. Okay? I am sorry. *(Silence.)*

PEG. We should ... go meet Janelle.

GUNNER. Who's that?

PEG. Janelle. I told you. She's the woman we're meeting. She's the guest coordinator.

GUNNER. "Guest?" Like we're on vacation?

PEG. I want you to —

GUNNER. Like a roach motel. Ya check in but ya don't check out. *(The lights fade on Gunner, rise on Peg and Jack.)*

PEG. If you back me up on this —

JACK. God —

PEG. I need your help here, Jack. We'll do it together. He'll listen to you.

JACK. Since when?

PEG. Something has to be done.

JACK. I can't force him.

PEG. Fine. He can move in with you.

JACK. I don't even live there anymore.

PEG. That's just temporary.

JACK. No, it's not.

PEG. All couples —

JACK. Mom, I moved out. We've got lawyers, okay? We're this close to wrapping it all up. Will you please accept this? *(Silence.)*

PEG. Well ... what did you do?

JACK. Oh, it's automatically me —

PEG. It's usually the husband, yes. That's a proven fact. Men are ... *(A beat.)* Just ... men. What about Barb?

JACK. What about her, Mom?

PEG. Do I still have ... visitation rights?

JACK. Of course.

PEG. Because I ... adore that girl —

JACK. I know —

PEG. Barb has always been such a — a ...

JACK. A saint, I know, I know. The Vatican calls twice a week. *(Silence; Peg sighs.)* It's nobody's fault, Mom. Okay?

PEG. It's always somebody's fault —

JACK. Then call the Guinness book folks because we're the first —

PEG. Then why?

JACK. I don't know.

PEG. That's not an answer.

JACK. That's all I got, Mom.

PEG. Okay. *(Geese are heard in the distance. Jack looks out for a moment.)*

JACK. Maybe ... we're both just ... hittin' fifty and — you know ... I mean, come on — what did we know? — we were kids.

PEG. So were Dad and I.

JACK. No comment.

PEG. Don't be fresh.

JACK. Kevin and Connie are out. Tim goes next year. If we can ever get him out of his room. And Barb and I both just — the thought of ... being alone. Just us. Just us in that house. Just us. Every night. It's kind of ... terrifying. During the day we're at work — no problem. Night, God. Night. Two of us sitting there — TV on — nothing to say. Her watching endless *Gilmore Girls* reruns. No thanks.

PEG. A lot of people manage.

JACK. Well, good for them. I mean, if the kids were still there it'd be ... *(His voice trails off.)* You know, I think we have kids so that we have something to talk about in restaurants. Barb and I would go out to dinner and ... the whole evening — that's all we talked about. That or silence. At home at least we could ... go into another room. Not when you're out. Kids. The whole conversation.

PEG. Have you thought about the church?

JACK. Not in years. Why?

PEG. You stood there in front of Father Edward and took a vow.

JACK. He out of jail yet?

PEG. Don't start —

18

JACK. Is he? *(A beat.)*

PEG. No. *(She picks up the brochures.)* Are you going to help me with this?

JACK. Mom, please — I got enough goin' on at the moment.

PEG. I'm sorry if our timing is inconvenient. And … and I'm sorry you're having your … problems. Problems, I have to be honest, I don't understand but you seem to … *(Her voice trails off as lights begin to dim.)* I'm sorry, Jack, I just … I don't … understand a lot of things anymore. And I'm just going to … miss Barb, I guess. She was like my daughter. *(Lights rise on Gunner on the beach.)*

GUNNER. Never really liked that woman.

JACK. I know.

GUNNER. I was polite all these years. Right? I wasn't rude or anything.

JACK. You were overly polite. That's how I knew you didn't like her.

GUNNER. Always got the feeling she was kind of … lookin' down her nose at me.

JACK. Good call. I mean, she liked you but, you know, her family —

GUNNER. I can smell people, Jack. *(Jack's heard this a few times.)*

JACK. I know.

GUNNER. When you deal with Teamsters you gotta be —

JACK and GUNNER. — three steps ahead of the other guy.

GUNNER. Absolutely right. *(Begins reeling in.)* You were too young to get — *(He stops suddenly. The word won't come. He stands a moment, frustrated.)*

JACK. Married?

GUNNER. Yeah — married.

JACK. Didn't seem to bother you at the time.

GUNNER. Figured she was knocked up like your mother was. *(This is a major bombshell. Jack stands there, waiting for the punchline. None comes. Gunner inspects his bait.)* Not even nibblin' today. Too cold.

JACK. Wait a minute. Wait a minute … what did you just say?

GUNNER. Not bitin'. Season's over.

JACK. No, no, no. About Mom.

GUNNER. I don't know. What'd I say?

JACK. That — I mean, was … was Mom … pregnant with me when you guys got married?

GUNNER. Why ya think we did it? *(Off Jack's look.)* What —

19

you didn't know this?

JACK. No, I didn't know this. No one ever told me.

GUNNER. Well how'd you want us ta bring it up? "Hey, Jack, ya cute little bastard. Oh, speakin' of that … "

JACK. *(Suddenly wary.)* Don't yank my chain here, Dad. I'm not in the mood.

GUNNER. I'm not yankin' anything, Jack. God's truth. *(Jack studies his father and finally decides to believe him.)*

JACK. Jesus …

GUNNER. Assumed ya knew.

JACK. No.

GUNNER. You never sat down and did the math?

JACK. I never thought I had to! My parents told me something — take that back, Mom told me something and I believed it. Jesus …

GUNNER. Christ, no big deal. Back then — our neighborhood — all the time.

JACK. But … I mean, come on … it's … Mom. Mom. My mom. I mean … I got this whole … thing in my head. The pictures and everything. The whole … good Catholic girl thing —

GUNNER. Hey, Catholic girls were pistols, lemme tell ya. There was an Italian girl over on Eighth Street —

JACK. Dad, Dad — no. Okay? Just … no. Not … the time. *(Jack wanders away and sits on the steps, still figuring things out.)*

GUNNER. You were actually a — whatta ya call it — fluke. Serious. After you were born, doctor told your mom she … ya know — she wasn't … "built" to have kids. Million to one shot. You were a lottery ticket, we'd all be rich. *(Gunner sits next to him.)* Ya know your mother was … God, she was beautiful.

JACK. I remember —

GUNNER. Grace Kelly beautiful. Used to be real quiet too, ya know. Wouldn't say boo. Kid you not. My mother thought she was a little "slow." We'd go out — Saturday night — party or somethin' and she'd just sit there. *(Lights rise on Peg. Party sounds and music can be heard in the background. Throughout most of this Peg's eyes are glued to the ground, embarrassed.)* And yeah, okay, it was kind of a rough crowd. Guys from the neighborhood. Truckers. Salvy, you know.

PEG. They just ignore me.

GUNNER. 'Cause you never say anything, baby. You gotta make some noise.

PEG. I never know what to say.

GUNNER. You talk to me.

PEG. That's different. Your friends are … so …

GUNNER. Loud. *(She laughs.)* That's all they are, Peggy.

PEG. I just … feel stupid sometimes.

GUNNER. Are you kiddin' me? You might be goin' to college — *(Peg tries to say something but Gunner plows on, pointing around the room.)* — and these clowns — I mean, Jimmy's a nice guy but I seen smarter door knobs. He wore loafers till high school 'cause he couldn't work the laces. *(She laughs.)* And Salvy's no Einstein —

PEG. *(Blurting.)* I got in. *(This quiets him down.)* I uhh — got the letter today. I got accepted.

GUNNER. Why didn't ya say somethin'?

PEG. Not here —

GUNNER. Yo — yo! Shut up a second. Peg got into college! *(She reacts a bit awkwardly to shouts of "congratulations.")* College, Jimmy. It's what some people do after high school, knucklehead. *(Back to Peg.)* You're gonna be a great teacher.

PEG. First grade, I decided. I really want to — I want to be their first, you know. Teach them to read. Like Sister Anne did with me. She was so wonderful and you never forget that.

GUNNER. I didn't have her. I had Sister what's-er-name — the one with the moustache. *(Peg laughs. He strokes her hair and she enjoys the moment, but her eyes suddenly go to the floor and she appears to shrink a bit. Gunner feels it instinctively.)* What's wrong?

PEG. I don't know. Little scary, I guess.

GUNNER. What's scary?

PEG. *(A mumble.)* I don't know. Everything. College. What if I'm not smart enough? What if I'm … I don't know … just once I want to be really … good at something.

GUNNER. You're good at bein' beautiful. *(She smiles but her eyes stay glued to the floor.)* What's on your shoes? You got the sports page down there? Must be somethin' good 'cause that's where you been lookin' all night. And stop mumblin', babe. *(He gently touches her chin, moving her face to his.)* Look people right in the eye and say your piece. And if somebody interrupts, say it louder. You're gonna be a teacher one'a these days. Maybe a principal. You gotta learn to do this or those kids'll run all over ya. *(The lights fade on her.)* Shy people get eaten alive … *(Lights out on Peg as Gunner turns to Jack.)* Woman hasn't shut up since. Go figure. Swear ta God. I hadda quiet one and screwed it all up. Talks to strangers inna supermarket. Gonna end up onna side of a milk carton one a these days. Women can't stand silence. Me and Salvy go fishin' for five hours, not say a word 'cept, "Gimme a — " *(Gunner stops. Again, he can't remember the word. Jack waits, then sees Gunner silently struggling.)*

JACK. Beer?

GUNNER. Jesus. Of all the words ta forget, huh? *(He forces a laugh but is clearly embarrassed.)* So … the restaurant gonna be okay with you not bein' there? *(Jack turns, curious.)*

JACK. What?

GUNNER. How they run things without ya? You got like a back-up chef or somethin'? 'Cause when the boss is away that's when the stealin' starts —

JACK. *(Gently.)* I don't own a restaurant, dad. Haven't even worked in one since high school. *(Gunner says nothing, processing this.)*

GUNNER. Right … right … I, uhhh … *(He suddenly hits himself in the head with his fist.)* Goddamnit! *(Jack says nothing, letting the frustration subside. Finally, Gunner forces a smile and points to his head.)* My brain's gettin' like your Uncle Mike. It only works occasionally. Restaurant … Jesus … *(A beat.)* Hey, ya know what'd be good? Some'a your pancakes. Whatta ya say — tomorrow morning? You still make good pancakes?

JACK. Haven't in a while. Barb doesn't eat 'em and Tim … he has like … Pop-Tarts or something.

GUNNER. No wonder he's so fat. *(Off Jack's look.)* Hey, I'm sorry. I know I'm s'posed to say … "glandular" or … "eating challenged" or something but let's face it — the kid is fat.

JACK. I know.

GUNNER. What's his problem? *(Jack shrugs.)* He got any plans?

JACK. *(A disgusted sigh.)* He wants to design video games. Him and every other kid in America.

GUNNER. Any money in that?

JACK. For one out of every billion kids, yeah. Rest of 'em end up livin' in their parents' basement.

GUNNER. He pouts alla time. Like somebody just stole his sandwich or somethin'. Looks like you when he does that. *(Off Jack's look.)* When you were a kid. You usta gimme that look. He's like a fat version a you sometimes.

JACK. Yeah, well … hopefully he'll grow out of it.

GUNNER. You did. Whatta ya say — make some pancakes tomorrow?

JACK. Sure. *(Silence.)*

GUNNER. Heard ya on the phone today. You got a woman law-yer? 'Cause you could use Dave, ya know —

JACK. I'd rather —

GUNNER. All the business I've thrown him he'd cut ya a deal.

JACK. No thanks, Dad. She's very competent.

GUNNER. Yeah, well — that's uhh ... probably smart. Inna divorce thing. Looks good. So ... how's it goin'?

JACK. *(A shrug.)* It's going.

GUNNER. She fightin' ya?

JACK. Couple small things. About the house mostly. Nothing major.

GUNNER. She'll be okay for money, right?

JACK. She makes more than I do.

GUNNER. A man takes care'a his family.

JACK. She'll be fine. *(Gunner nods, accepting this. Silence.)*

GUNNER. I'm ... glad ya came down. Short notice, I know, callin' ya like that —

JACK. I got a ton of vacation time.

GUNNER. Yeah, well, I appreciate it. *(Silence; Gunner's unsure how to proceed.)* Listen, do me a favor.

JACK. Okay.

GUNNER. And I'm serious here. This is not the crazy-old-man talkin' here. I know I slipped on the restaurant thing —

JACK. Dad —

GUNNER. But I know what I'm doin' here. And you can't tell Mom. *(Jack sighs.)* Jesus, don't you start that too.

JACK. What?

GUNNER. That sighhhh. Like somebody ice-picked a tire.

JACK. Sorry.

GUNNER. Look, I want you to call your lawyer. Tell her whatever deal's on the table you will accept it today —

JACK. What're you doing —

GUNNER. No more negotiations. Barb gets whatever she wants. But it's a one day offer. Today. That's it. Her lawyer FedExes us a binding deal memo —

JACK. Dad —

GUNNER. Don't interrupt — I might get crazy. A binding deal memo today spelling out everything. It has to be signed and nota-rized. We get it tomorrow morning, you sign and notarize — and

23

FedEx it back. It's a sweet deal for her. But it has to be done today.

JACK. Who knows if she'll even agree —

GUNNER. Jack, I negotiated with Teamsters, remember? And I always come outta the room with my pants still on. You make her this offer, she'll take it.

JACK. Why would I do this? We're talkin' a few grand here. I can use that money —

GUNNER. I'll cover it. You gotta trust me —

JACK. I do, I just —

GUNNER. No ya don't. You think I'm nuts.

JACK. No —

GUNNER. Yes ya do and I don't blame ya but — listen to me. *(Desperate.)* Please, you gotta — I don't know how many good days I got left. Your mother's out at Wal-Mart pricin' diapers for me. I gotta lotta stuff I gotta do and — and this is one of 'em. It's a ... loose end. Can't have any loose ends. Please, please ... do it.

JACK. Why's it got to be today —

GUNNER. It just does, okay?

JACK. Not gonna take much longer —

GUNNER. Okay, how much? How much are we talkin' here? The difference. Ballpark figure.

JACK. I don't —

GUNNER. Ballpark figure!

JACK. I don't know. Twenty grand, maybe. *(Heading for the house.)*

GUNNER. I'll write you a — a — goddamnit! *(Again, he can't find the word.)*

JACK. Check.

GUNNER. Check! I'll write you a — how much? Twenty? Thirty — if I give ya thirty will ya —

JACK. Why?

GUNNER. *(Exploding.) Will you just fucking trust me please?!* (He immediately pulls back, glancing at the house.)

JACK. She's not home.

GUNNER. Thank God. *(Moving to Jack.)* This ... *(Points to his head.)* I feel like it's startin' ta show. Like, like ... chicken pox or somethin'. I go to the grocery store — and I'm not droolin' or acting nutty or anything — but I swear people can ... smell it on me or somethin'. "There's crazy old Gunner. Sure hope he doesn't take a leak in the produce section or somethin'." I'm embarrassed and I'm not even doin' anything. She talked to you 'bout that place right?

JACK. Yes.

GUNNER. She show ya that damn brochure she carries around everywhere? You should see this place. *(Gunner reels in his line.)*

JACK. I did. *(Off his look.)* She asked me to.

GUNNER. And?

JACK. For what it is, it's nice —

GUNNER. You know how much they want for that place? And ya don't own it. You croak, they put ya on a conveyor belt and bring in the next one. They're hopin' ya die quick. Turnover.

JACK. I don't think that's —

GUNNER. And they can jack it up on ya, up ta four percent. Every damn year if they want. Screw them. *(The light changes back to the warm glow of the assisted living place. The music plays softly as Peg appears.)* No way in hell I'm endin' up there …

PEG. We have to meet Janelle.

GUNNER. Who's Janelle?

PEG. I just told you —

GUNNER. *(Moving away.)* What's down here?

PEG. We're late, Gunner —

GUNNER. This part over here —

PEG. We don't have to see that — *(The music suddenly stops and the lights give a cold, sterile glare. They are in the A-Wing.)*

GUNNER. Jeezus Christ …

PEG. *(Gently.)* This is the … personal care ward.

GUNNER. *(Inhaling.)* Lysol and shit. Smells like a Holiday Inn.

PEG. Gunner, please —

GUNNER. You know how much they want for this place?

PEG. Yes, I know, Gunner. I am not a complete idiot. I know how much.

GUNNER. Oh, look what's for lunch. Jello. What a racket. *(He moves away.)*

PEG. Gunner, you can't just go into the —

GUNNER. Sayin' hello to my future roommates. *(He leans into a room.)* Hey, how's it goin', pal? *(No reaction from the patient.)* Not much of a talker, huh. Boy, he's gonna be fun ta watch a game with. *(Turns to Peg.)* Christ … lookit this poor bastard. He's a vegetable, Peg. Somebody should just stamp "Bird's Eye" on him.

PEG. *(Controlling.)* We need to see Janelle.

GUNNER. Get a better conversation from those machines —

PEG. Gunner, please.

GUNNER. Wonder how much they cost —

PEG. Damnit, Gunner — *(He reacts to her language.)*

GUNNER. Great, Peg. Now we gotta stop at confession onna way home.

PEG. *(Repressing the rage.)* What … do … you want me to do?

GUNNER. Whatever the hell ya want but leave me out of it.

PEG. Will you please just meet with Janelle —

GUNNER. Who's Janelle?

PEG. I just — *(Restraining.)* She's … the guest coordinator.

GUNNER. Peg, do you really think I'm gonna end up like that poor guy? Layin' there like that? *(Lights begin to fade on Peg.)* Answer me, Peg. And be honest. Be honest. Do ya? *(Lights return to normal.)*

JACK. *(Delicately.)* So what's Mom gonna do?

GUNNER. I'll tell ya exactly what she's gonna do. She's gonna cry and wail and wear black and enjoy every damned minute of it. She'll finally get ta be a martyr. They'll start sellin' little plastic statues of Peg you can put on your dashboard. *(Jack tries to suppress the laugh, but can't. Gunner joins in.)*

JACK. Jesus, Dad, that's terrible. *(He starts laughing again.)*

GUNNER. Am I lyin'?

JACK. No, but —

GUNNER. If I'm lyin', I'm dyin'. *(Off Jack's look.)* Sorry. *(Silence.)* I didn't work my ass off my whole life ta give everything away to a buncha doctors. When I'm gone she can do whatever the hell she wants. Sell this place. Move back to the city, I don't care. Till then I'm still runnin' things. Still the boss.

JACK. She's not a truck, Dad.

GUNNER. Wish she was. I understand trucks. *(Inspecting the bait.)* Too damn cold. *(He puts the rod in a holder, done for the day.)* Call that lawyer, will ya? And for God's sake do-not-tell-your-mother. *(Lights fade on Gunner and rise on Peg.)*

PEG. So what did he say?

JACK. About what?

PEG. What I asked you to talk to him about.

JACK. What do you think he said, Mom?

PEG. Well, I'm all out of ideas. Maybe you can think of something.

JACK. What other options are there?

PEG. Your father's first suggestion was a murder-suicide pact. I said no thank you. Knowing him, he'd shoot me, then forget to shoot himself. *(On reflex Jack tries to stifle his laugh. Peg's reaction says, "It's* okay." *Even she finds a little humor in it and they share a quiet laugh. Silence. Then Peg sits, exhausted.)* The first time I went there the woman who — Janelle, I told you — she — well, the first thing she said to me was that I shouldn't feel guilty. And it kind of threw me. I said, "Guilty about what?" I mean, am I missing something? Why should I feel guilty? What are my options? I'm doing the right thing. *(As if convincing herself.)* It's not like I'm dumping him in a warehouse or something. I'll be there every day. Every day. *(Lights begin to fade on them.)* He's my husband and I intend to take … care of him. *(Lights out on Peg and Jack as they rise on Gunner, who has his back to us. We hear the sound of a truck pulling away. Gunner waves to it.)*

GUNNER. Thanks again! *(Gunner now turns front and we see he holds a FedEx envelope. He stares at it a moment, looking a little unsure, then looks skyward as if in a very brief silent prayer. He tears it open, puts on his glasses, and reads the contents carefully.)* Yes! *(He lets out a happy laugh and does a little dance.)* Yes, yes, yes! *(Gunner slows down, breathing a little heavily but still smiling. He glances back at the house to see if anybody has seen his celebration. Coast clear. He carefully replaces the papers into the envelope. Then, as if something kind of serious has crossed his mind, he looks out at the water, deep in thought. But only for a moment. He shakes it off, shoves the envelope under his shirt, and heads towards the house. As the lights fade on Gunner they rise on Peg and Jack in the kitchen. Jack reads a copy of* Philadelphia *magazine. It is night, after dinner.)*

PEG. What's the secret? *(Off his look.)* That lamb. Best I ever had. Melt in your mouth. How'd you do it?

JACK. Marinate.

PEG. I marinate.

JACK. Yeah, for like ten minutes. Twenty-four hours at least, Mom.

PEG. Who has that sort of time? *(Jack pulls out his cell, reading a text.)*

JACK. You don't sit there and watch it. *(Re: text.)* Tim.

PEG. Anything important?

JACK. No. Just his nightly, "I-hate-you-why-was-I-born" stuff. *(He pockets the phone and moves to the counter, picking up some olive oil.)*

PEG. Why is that boy so angry all the time? Kevin and Connie are so perfect.

JACK. Maybe that's why.

PEG. Well, they are. *(She watches as he pours some olive oil on his*

27

hand and twists his wedding ring.)

JACK. Yeah, but are they "perfect" because they wanted to be or … they thought it'd make Barb and me happy?

PEG. What're you doing?

JACK. Trying to get this ring off. I tried soap, moisturizer — *(Gunner enters carrying a bottle of whiskey.)*

PEG. Do you have to do that now?

JACK. No. I just saw the olive oil and thought it might —

GUNNER. You'll hafta cut it off, Jack. The ring — not your finger. *(Holds up his ring finger.)* Never taken this off, have I, Peg. Skin probably looks like a piece a veal. Make sure the undertaker gives it to ya. Get a couple bucks. *(With a flourish he puts the bottle on the table.)* Who's ready for dessert?

JACK. I made creme brulée.

GUNNER. Brought my own. Middleton. Distilled in East Cork, Ireland. Your great-grandfather worked in the distillery. It is the finest — bar none — whiskey on the planet. Guy at the liquor store had to order it for me. Smell that.

PEG. You know I don't like the smell.

JACK. My God, that is wonderful. I could make a sauce with this you wouldn't —

GUNNER. You do and I'll break your arm. *(Puts glasses on the table.)* Aged twenty-five years. You drink this neat. No water no ice. Okay?

JACK. Pour. *(As he pours carefully.)*

GUNNER. Only had this once. Day I sold the business to Berger. Pulls a bottle out of his — *(He loses the word. Peg immediately, gently, fills in.)*

PEG. Desk.

GUNNER. Desk as we signed the papers. A Jewish guy gimme the best glass of Irish whiskey I ever had. Go figure.

JACK. *(Sipping.)* Ohhh … that is nice, dad.

GUNNER. Two hundred and forty bucks, it better be.

PEG. How much?

GUNNER. You heard me.

PEG. Are you out of your mind?

GUNNER. Not at the moment. Stick around, ya never know.

PEG. Two hundred and forty dollars for a … a … bottle of booze.

GUNNER. An *excellent* bottle of booze. Worth every penny. We are celebrating!

PEG. What in the world is there to celebrate? *(Jack shoots Gunner a "Don't push this" look — assuming he knows where his father is going.)*
GUNNER. No more loose ends, that's what. A huge … huge weight has been lifted! Hallelujah! I haven't felt this good in — who knows? Who cares? It feels good! Go figure.
PEG. Gunner —
GUNNER. Saw the FedEx guy pull up —
PEG. What was FedEx doing —
JACK. Dad —
GUNNER. Started dancin' like Fred Astaire — Hello, FedEx guy! Wanted to kiss him on the lips.
PEG. *(Sharp.)* Gunner! *(Silence.)* Focus, Gunner. Focus. Who am I? *(Gunner smiles. He knows he'll pass the test this time.)*
GUNNER. Richard Nixon.
PEG. Gunner — *(He reaches out happily and takes her hands.)*
GUNNER. You are Margaret Constance O'Rourke. You lived at 342 Tasker Avenue. I met you on March 12th, cold day. You'd just come out of Finnegan's Drug Store with your cousin, Shirley. You both had Saint Agnes uniforms. Shirley had a Hershey Bar. You were drinkin' a Coke with a straw. Piece'a your hair was stuck to the corner of your mouth. And you were the most beautiful girl I ever saw in my life. *(Silence. Peg finally smiles.)*
PEG. It was a Dr. Pepper.
GUNNER. You sure? *(She nods.)* Okay, but that was pretty good though, wasn't it?
PEG. It was very good.
GUNNER. *(Gripping her hand.)* I'm not on the Looneyville Trolley right now, Peg. Trust me.
PEG. Okay. I'm sorry, I just — what is it we're celebrating, Gunner? Don't get me wrong, I would love something to celebrate —
GUNNER. Decisions have been made. Loose ends tied up. Weights lifted.
PEG. *(Confused.)* Yes, you said —
GUNNER. First, you should be very proud of our son. *(Jack looks uncomfortable.)*
PEG. Okay. Why?
GUNNER. Because he did the right thing. He gave Barb everything she wanted. Didn't fight a thing.
PEG. Is this why you're trying to get your ring off —
GUNNER. Stop there, Peg.

PEG. And that is ... cause for celebration? Not to mention a two-hundred and forty dollar bottle of —

GUNNER. Money is no object. Not tonight. Not tonight. *(Pulls a paper out of his pocket.)* I wrote it down. An agenda. Just in case I ... *(Spins his finger next to his head indicating "nuts." Jack shakes his empty glass.)*

JACK. May I?

GUNNER. Don't go nuts. I got plans for that. *(He's forgotten something.)* Damn. Right back. *(He exits.)*

PEG. I thought you still had some things to iron out.

JACK. *(Avoiding.)* They got ironed out.

PEG. Just like that?

JACK. Just like that.

PEG. What's going on?

JACK. How should I know?

PEG. You two — out on the beach all day. The boat. And you hate the beach and the boat. Now what is he — *(But she stops as Gunner enters with a manila envelope.)*

GUNNER. Okay, okay — we got stuff to do and as president of the family the floor is mine. *(With a touch of ceremony he places the envelope on the table.)* Everything is in there. Everything you are going to need. *(Off their looks.)* Money. We're talkin' money here. 'Cause we gotta tie everything up. Now we've all been over the will —

PEG. Not this again.

GUNNER. Oh, yeah — there's ten grand in the freezer.

PEG. What?

GUNNER. Ten grand, backa the freezer. *(Peg leaps up and runs offstage.)* Wrapped up in aluminum foil inna plastic bag — *(To Jack.)* What's her problem?

PEG. *(Offstage.)* Thank God! *(She reenters looking relieved.)* I thought I threw it out.

GUNNER. Why would ya do that?

PEG. Because I clean out the freezer once in a while. Why don't you tell people about these things?

GUNNER. That's what I'm doin' now.

JACK. Why'd you have ten grand in the freezer?

GUNNER. Emergency, I don't know. And if you're a burglar you gonna look through the freezer?

PEG. *(Resigned.)* Okay, okay.

GUNNER. That's yours, Peg. Some "walkin' around money." Now

everything else is pretty well set up and it'll keep comin'. 'Tween the 401(k)s, the investments, Social Security — those bastards — you're set, Peg. For life. Anything ya want.

PEG. I know all this, Gunner. And I'm really not comfortable talking —

GUNNER. We gotta do this. *(Before she can react.)* Now.

PEG. What is the hurry? Your heart is in excellent condition, Gunner. You passed your cancer screening —

GUNNER. I'm goin' crazy —

PEG. Stop calling it that. You are in excellent shape — besides that — and … and … you've got at least — at least — a good ten, fifteen years.

GUNNER. I may have 'em but they ain't gonna be good.

PEG. Jack, do you want to listen to this?

JACK. Will you stop doing that, please?

PEG. *(Too innocent.)* What?

JACK. Puttin' me in these "no win" situations. *(Rising abruptly.)* I agree with him, you're pissed; I agree with you, he's pissed. *(He suddenly reacts in pain and grabs his neck.)*

PEG. What is it?

GUNNER. What'sa matter? You okay?

JACK. My neck — the pinched nerve —

PEG. What did you do?

JACK. I stood up! That's all I — owwww …

PEG. I'll get some ibuprofen.

JACK. Just please stop, okay … putting me in the middle all the time.

GUNNER. Jack, nothin' personal but I don't give a rat's ass what anybody says I'm doin' this. *(Pulling out papers.)* Now, this is the good part … *(Peg silently rolls her eyes at that description as Gunner sorts things out. She hands Jack water and Ibuprofen.)* Need a little drum roll here … *(Lays the papers on the table.)* The life insurance. One-point-two million dollars. *(Peg and Jack are both silently stunned.)*

PEG. A … million-two?

JACK. Wow …

PEG. You never — why on earth did you have that much —

GUNNER. When the business started takin' off, Peg, I was in debt up ta here. Somethin' happened to me, you and Jack were stuck with it. This was ta take care of you. Wipe out the debt and still have somethin' ta live on. Dave set it all up for me. These

31

things been paid off for years. *(He pats the policies.)* One-point-two million. You and Jack are co-beneficiaries, right down a middle. Now, a million-two on toppa what you already have, Peg — you're sittin' pretty. But … you can both be sittin' prettier. *(Perusing the policy.)* Read it, will ya. That print's ridiculous.

JACK. "If cause of death is the result of accident — see exclusions section two subheading A — beneficiary shall be paid double face value of the policy."

GUNNER. And those exclusions are war, "in the process of committing an illegal act" and crashing in a non-commercial airplane. *(A beat.)* Two-point-four million bucks for an accidental death. *(He waits for a reaction. Finally:)*

PEG. So?

GUNNER. So? So I'm gonna die accidently that's what's "so." *(He makes a toast and sips his whiskey.)*

PEG. This is not funny.

GUNNER. Tell me about it.

JACK. Dad, what're you doing here?

GUNNER. I'm takin' care'a this while I still can, that's what I'm doin' —

PEG. *(Rising.)* Gilmore Girls are on.

GUNNER. You want to hear this or not?

PEG. No.

GUNNER. Fine. I'll tell Jack. He'll tell you. *(A stand-off. Finally she sits.)* Now, let's be honest here. You got a better chance of seein' Christ-direct-traffic-with-a-cigar-in-his-mouth than you got of gettin' me into that home.

PEG. It's not a —

GUNNER. It is too! It's a damn warehouse with a swimmin' pool. No way —

PEG. Then what do you suggest we —

GUNNER. Jesus Christ, lemme finish, will ya? *(Softening.)* Come on, Peg. You seen every one of those *Gilmore Girls*. Just gimme a minute. *(Peg lets out one of her sighs.)* I knew it! I knew you'd do that!

PEG. Can we get this over with? Please?

GUNNER. Two-point-four million's a helluva lot better'n one-point-two. *(Before Peg can react.)* Don't say a word — it's not stealin'. After what they charged me all these years? So lay off the Ten Commandment thing. It don't count with insurance companies.

PEG. So what are you planning to do, Gunner? Throw yourself

32

down the steps?

GUNNER. Hell no. That'd hurt.

PEG. *(To Jack.)* Are you just going to sit there? *(Before Jack can react.)*

GUNNER. Whatta ya want him to do? Card tricks? He's listening. You should try it.

PEG. Okay, okay, okay. Just tell us what you're doing and we'll call it a night.

GUNNER. I'm gonna drown. Okay? Fall outta the boat. Glub, glub. Go watch your show. *(Silence. Gunner sips his drink.)*

PEG. *(Rising.)* Fine.

GUNNER. Tomorrow night.

PEG. Whatever.

GUNNER. *(To Jack.)* I knew she'd do that. *(Peg exits.)* Okay, tomorrow night, tide starts goin' out around six —

JACK. Dad, hold up a sec —

GUNNER. What?

JACK. Come on, you pushed it far enough.

GUNNER. Jack, I'm not kiddin' here —

JACK. Since when. Dad, you got a track record here, okay — *(Off Gunner's look.)* We can start with the alligator out there and work our way up if you want. Come on …

GUNNER. Jesus, I'm tellin' the truth. All thought out. Wrote it all down 'case … ya know … *(Points to his head.)* Now, every night 'bout that time — like you and me tonight — I been takin' a little cruise inna boat. All the neighbors see me. They'll swear to it in court if they have to. Clockwork. Tomorrow night — same time, same station — I head out. Alone. *(Points to the whiskey.)* Well, me and him. Head south downa canal. Full moon, so the tide's gonna be crazy goin' out. Finish that bottle. Keep the boat runnin'. Over the side I go. Only take a minute. No pain, no strain. Two-point-four million bucks. Take your half — open a restaurant — go ta Tahiti — whatever ya want.

JACK. Okay. *(A beat.)*

GUNNER. Jesus Christ — why won't you believe me?

JACK. 'Cause I'm tired of bein' the sucker — okay, Dad? You been doin' this to me my whole life — I'm not fallin' for it — *(Peg steps out of the shadows.)*

PEG. He's telling the truth. *(Moving to Gunner.)* You are — aren't you. I know you —

33

GUNNER. Hallelujah …

PEG. No —

GUNNER. Yes —

PEG. No. I won't allow it.

GUNNER. Whatta ya gonna do? Ground me?

PEG. I'll — I'll take the boat keys.

GUNNER. You don't know where they are.

PEG. Neither will you by tomorrow.

GUNNER. I-am-not-wearin'-diapers goddamnit! I'm not gonna lay there not knowin' anybody, not — no, forget about it. Not me. Not so a buncha doctors can line their wallets. "Quality of life." Kiss my ass. Oh, almost forgot. *(Pulls a pill bottle from his pocket.)* I'll take a couple of these too as a chaser. Oxy … *(Jack grabs them.)*

JACK. Oxy-Contin?

GUNNER. Took one for my back a couple weeks ago. I was droolin'. Knock ya right out.

PEG. Where did you get those?

JACK. *(Reading the label.)* Salvy.

GUNNER. He don't need 'em anymore.

JACK. Can I have one of these — *(Off Peg's look.)* My neck.

PEG. You just took ibuprofen.

GUNNER. *(Hands him some pills.)* Here. Take a couple.

PEG. You don't take other people's pills.

GUNNER. Try 'em with a little whiskey. *(Peg reaches for the bottle as Jack pockets the pills.)*

PEG. Give me those.

GUNNER. Get your own. *(Shoving them in his pocket.)* And don't even think about it. I'll hide them too. So … a couple'a these … little whiskey. I slow the boat down like I got up to check on somethin'. "Old guy falls out of movin' boat." Happens more'n ya think down here. And every neighbor'll swear I never wore a life jacket in my life.

PEG. So … so … you're just going to float away. That's your plan.

GUNNER. With a good tide I'll make it to Baltimore.

PEG. And, and — what if a little boy or girl finds your body? Think about that? They'd be traumatized.

GUNNER. Find a dead body? You kiddin'? They'd be the most popular kids in school.

PEG. *(With difficulty.)* And what about hell?

GUNNER. Been there. It's called A-Wing.

PEG. Suicide is a mortal sin.

GUNNER. So's molestin' kids. I'll be surrounded by priests.

PEG. This is not some damn joke! *(Simultaneously.)*

GUNNER. Believe me, I know it —

JACK. Mom — come on —

PEG. *(It bursts out.)* Then why didn't you just do it?! Why are you telling us?! Why do we have to listen to — Why do we have to be in on it? *(A beat. For the first time Gunner looks a bit sheepish.)*

GUNNER. 'Cause … I didn't wanta … look like … some sorta idiot or somethin'. "Old feeble-brained Gunner — crazy old man fell outta his boat." I wanted ya to know … that I … that I knew what I was doin'. *(Silence.)* Didn't wanta … embarrass myself anymore in fronta ya, Peg. *(Quietly.)* Hate that. God, I … worst part 'bout this whole thing, I swear. Never knowin' when I'm gonna … make an ass outta myself. Burn the house down … *(Sips his drink, forces a smile and turns to Jack.)* So whatta ya think, huh? This time tomorrow night you're a millionaire. *(They wait. Peg is very curious as to his reaction. Jack still looks dazed.)*

JACK. Why does it have to be … tomorrow?

GUNNER. You see any other boats still out there? Winter's comin'.

JACK. *(Floundering.)* So … so … you — it just has to be tomorrow —

GUNNER. I don't have a lotta time here, Jack! I'm startin' to lose it. Every day I — I … it gets … *(His voice trails off.)* I just gotta do this while I still can. *(Silence.)*

PEG. *(Quietly.)* No. *(Growing louder.)* No, no, no, no, no. You are not doing this!

GUNNER. Please, Peg. You promised —

PEG. No —

GUNNER. Saint Paddy's Day —

PEG. No —

GUNNER. Don't make it rough on me —

PEG. And what about me? I'm supposed to … to just … no, Gunner, no.

GUNNER. I just want your blessing —

PEG. *(Incredulous.)* "Blessing?"

GUNNER. I'm tryin' to take care'a you —

PEG. My blessing. Are you out of your mind?

GUNNER. Yes! Yes, Peg, I am! I didn't know my son! I tried to

watch *Cops* on the microwave for Christ's sake. And I can't do it anymore — not for another goddamned day! *(They both react to his outburst. Gunner reels it in, taking her hands.)* Just ... don't wantcha mad at me, Peg. Not anymore, please. I don't want anybody hatin' me so ... please, Peg, please just ... I'm beggin' ya ... say it's okay ... please, say it's okay ... *(He kisses her hands.)* Lemme off the hook ...
PEG. No.
GUNNER. You promised me —
PEG. I did no such thing —
GUNNER. You did — you know you did. Saint Paddy's Day, you —
PEG. *(Exploding.)* No! Are you listening to me, Gunner? You want me to give you some sort of ... of ... "okay" for this crazy — no. No! Forget it. No. *(Silence. He searches her face. It is set — cold. Gunner's face hardens.)*
GUNNER. Jesus, you must hate me ... *(They stare at each other a moment. Finally, Gunner lets go of her hands and begins to move away slowly.)* I'm goin' ta bed. *(To Jack.)* Talk to her. *(Gunner heads off, then stops, turning back.)* Jack ... tomorrow ... *(They wait as if for some pronouncement.)* Tomorrow ... could you ... make some pancakes? I'd really love some pancakes ... *(Without waiting for an answer Gunner trudges off. Jack finally turns to look at his mother. The lights fade.)*

End of Act One

ACT TWO

Lights rise on Jack. A glass of whiskey sits on the beach. He paces while on his cell.

JACK. Why didn't you hand it in? Don't give me that, Tim — you had how many weeks? What is so tough about getting in a term paper? No, you do not need a new computer — clean out the games and porn and yours is just fine … okay, whatever — flunk English — but don't cry to me when you can't get into wherever the hell it is you want to go — Tim? Tim don't — goddamnit … *(His tone softens as Tim hands the phone off.)* I don't know what to do, Barb. Ground him? He never leaves his room. Maybe we should force him to go outside. *(He listens.)* Yeah, I know, that was kind of sudden … well, thank you. And thank your lawyer. Don't believe I'm saying that. No, it's just … it's not … it's not … good here. Dad's … you know. Oh, and could you call Mom in the next couple days? She's all afraid you're gonna disown her. *(Lights rise on Gunner and Peg in two separate areas. Gunner wears an old baseball glove and holds another one.)* I know that, you know that — convince her you're still family, okay? *(Lights get brighter. It is day, years before. Gunner tosses Jack a glove.)*
PEG. Family is the most important thing in the world, Jacky.
GUNNER. Family is to be avoided at all costs. Which is tough on the holidays.
PEG. Family is always there for you —
GUNNER. Whether ya want 'em or not.
PEG. We will always be there for you, Jacky. No matter what. You remember that. *(Peg exits. Jack and Gunner begin to have a catch with an imaginary ball.)*
GUNNER. The problem with family is that you're expected to like 'em right off the bat. That's not natural. I mean, you want to like 'em. I wish I liked your Uncle Mike. But I shared a room with 'em and let me tell ya somethin', kid, he's a lazy, dishonest sack a crap. But because he's my brother I'm s'posed to overlook all that. Makes no sense. You gotta earn the right ta be liked. *(Moves to Jack,*

showing him how.) Block it on a grounder, Jack. Use your body to deaden the ball in case ya miss it. *(As Gunner moves back.)*

JACK. Why am I an only child?

GUNNER. What're you, the new priest?

JACK. I'm the only "only" kid in school.

GUNNER. You aren't an only child.

JACK. I'm not?

GUNNER. Noooo. We just kept you. *(Jack just stands there as the ball flies past him.)*

JACK. What?

GUNNER. Oh yeah. You had a couple brothers and sisters. Hadda sell 'em. Get the ball.

JACK. *(Incredulous.)* You ... sold them?

GUNNER. Got a nice price too. Good stock. Get the ball, son.

JACK. Who — who did you sell 'em to?

GUNNER. Couple went to a circus. Not Ringling Brothers — one'a the smaller ones. *(Jack is frozen so Gunner, enjoying this, gets the ball himself.)* One of them — 'member on TV, the Russians sent that dog into space? Now they're usin' babies. Got two hundred rubles for him. We'll probably see him on the news one'a these days. *(He gets a good look at the frightened kid.)* Relax. We're keepin' you. *(Moves back into place.)* Get ready. Hot grounder. *(Gunner throws — hard. Jack grabs his leg and crashes to the ground screaming out in pain.)* You're okay, Jack. Walk it off. *(Lights burst on above.)*

PEG. What happened?

GUNNER. Got nicked in the knee. He's fine.

PEG. He is not "fine."

GUNNER. It brushed him —

PEG. Jacky, come in the house —

GUNNER. Quit babyin' him.

PEG. Let's get some ice on that —

GUNNER. He's fine —

PEG. He's hurt —

GUNNER. He's not hurt. *(To Jack.)* Walk it off —

PEG. Come in the house, Jacky —

JACK. Did you sell babies?

PEG. Did I ... *(Realizing.)* What have you been telling him?

GUNNER. We were kiddin' around —

PEG. Are you out of your mind?

GUNNER. I was just —

PEG. Look at him! Does it look like he's in on the joke? Come in the house —

GUNNER. Stay outta this! He's fine.

PEG. Come on, Jacky.

GUNNER. Jesus Christ, Peg, will ya — (*Spins suddenly on Jack.*) Quit cryin' like a little girl, for Christ's sake.

PEG. Stop that!

GUNNER. Toughen up! Come on, knock it off!

PEG. Will you please let me —

GUNNER. Let you what, huh, Peg — what? Come on — what damnit? Put him in a little frilly apron and play restaurant? Two of ya in there in matching dresses baking your goddamn cupcakes. You're turnin' him into a three-dollar bill, for Chrise sake.

PEG. Will you please shut-up?

GUNNER. I'm embarrassed to be seen with this goddamn kid —

PEG. (*Sharp, angry.*) Gunner! (*The tone throws him. Jack looks confused as Gunner retreats.*)

GUNNER. You heard her. Go inna house. (*Gunner moves away, then stops a moment, turning back. He looks a bit repentant from his outburst.*) Jack? (*Gunner stands there a moment, unsure.*) Nothin', just … go inna house … (*Lights fade on Gunner.*)

PEG. You always ice an injury right away, Jacky. If you don't the bruise can go all the way down to the bone. (*As lights begin to fade on her.*) I knew a boy once who didn't put ice on it and ended up losing the whole leg. (*Jack looks out at the water. Quiet. He picks a few stones up off the shore and skims one, counting.*)

JACK. Two. Shit … (*He tries again — then winces in pain, grabbing his neck.*) Damnit! (*He drops the other stones to the beach, stands there a moment, then takes an Oxy-Contin out of his pocket, pops it, and washes it down with the whiskey as Peg steps outside.*)

PEG. He is sound asleep. Do you believe that? He makes this … this grand … proclamation. And now he's sleeping like a baby. I'm not going to sleep tonight. I doubt you are. But him he's … just … snoring away. Happy as a clam. (*She sits, looking out at the water, silence.*) What a stupid expression. (*Jack laughs quietly, moving to her.*) It makes no sense. Unless it's because — I mean, I suppose you could make a case that clams … look happy. That they look like they grin all the time.

JACK. That's not the whole expression.

PEG. It's not?

39

JACK. The whole expression is, "Happy as a clam at high tide."
PEG. I've never heard the "tide" part.
JACK. That's the whole thing. *(Peg thinks a moment.)*
PEG. Why would that make them happy?
JACK. No predators. Washed up on shore, they're vulnerable. Birds. Humans. End up in linguini with a nice white wine garlic sauce.
PEG. I don't know how people think those things up. Expressions.
JACK. Somebody has to. *(Silence.)*
PEG. He means it, you know.
JACK. That's what I was out here thinking about.
PEG. And? *(Jack says nothing, then shrugs.)* What was in the FedEx envelope?
JACK. Divorce stuff.
PEG. What? *(He says nothing, then sips his drink.)*
JACK. One thing I have never — never — said to my kids is, "Don't tell your mother."
PEG. I'm not following.
JACK. I wish I had a buck for every time you said, "Don't tell your father," and he said, "Don't tell your mother."
PEG. Pardon me for wanting to know what's going on in my family —
JACK. Mom …
PEG. I have had a lot thrown at me tonight, Jack. And I'm just trying to figure things out.
JACK. Okay, I'm sorry. *(Silence.)*
PEG. So what was in it?
JACK. You're killin' me here, Mom.
PEG. Not a great choice of words tonight.
JACK. Sorry.
PEG. Why is this such a state secret?
JACK. Okay, Dad suggested I kind of … expedite things. So I basically gave her everything she wanted. She signed off on it. For all intents and purposes I'm divorced. End of story.
PEG. Why would he want you to … *(Jack says nothing. Sips his drink.)* Is this why he called you? Why he wanted you down here? *(No reaction.)* Jack, is that why he —
JACK. I guess. I don't know.
PEG. Barb won't get any of the money. Will she? That's what this is all about — he doesn't want her to get —
JACK. Ask him —

PEG. Oh, you didn't think about that —

JACK. No, I didn't. He kept talkin' about "loose ends" and —

PEG. Never entered your mind —

JACK. *(Sharp.)* Hey, I've got other stuff on my mind tonight, okay? *(She observes him.)*

PEG. Are you drunk?

JACK. Not yet.

PEG. *(Rising.)* Then give me a hand before you get any worse.

JACK. With what?

PEG. The dinghy. *(She pulls a small flashlight from her jacket pocket and turns it on.)*

JACK. What're you doing, Mom?

PEG. I need to get out to the boat.

JACK. Why?

PEG. Are you going to help me or not?

JACK. Depends. *(Silence. She lets out one of her sighs.)*

PEG. Don't tell your father —

JACK. Oh, God …

PEG. — but I'm going to … keep it from starting tomorrow. Pull some wires or something.

JACK. That's crazy.

PEG. Oh, that's crazy. Drowning yourself is perfectly sane but this is —

JACK. I never said that! I just —

PEG. What do you want me to do, Jack? Come on — I'm open to suggestion —

JACK. I don't know —

PEG. Then help me, please. *(She heads down to the beach. He remains above.)* I have my pinking shears. I can … I can … cut a hose or something. Now come on —

JACK. And he'll go right down to the marina, buy another hose and —

PEG. Then I'll get a hammer —

JACK. Mom —

PEG. I'm not just gonna sit here, Jack —

JACK. Maybe you should.

PEG. I'll do it myself.

JACK. Fine. *(Peg exits. Jack watches, sipping his drink. We hear some grunts as Peg tries to pull the dinghy.)* Come on, Mom — you're gonna kill yourself —

PEG. *(Offstage.)* Not funny!

JACK. Sorry. *(Peg reenters.)*

PEG. Are you going to help or not?

JACK. Sit down a second. *(She stands there a moment, staring at him.)*

PEG. I don't … understand you at all tonight.

JACK. What?

PEG. You don't care if he kills himself.

JACK. Jesus, don't say that —

PEG. Looks that way.

JACK. I'm trying to figure some things out —

PEG. What's to figure out?

JACK. Mom, I've got no idea what it is I'm supposed to do here —

PEG. Well, I do! I am not just going to … I am not … ready … to lose my husband. *(Silence. Jack softens.)*

JACK. You've gotta … think of yourself here too, Mom —

PEG. I'll be fine.

JACK. *(Gently.)* It is not going to be easy … watching what's gonna happen eventually. What he's gonna turn into —

PEG. I never said it would be —

JACK. Do you really want to spend the rest of your life just … having to take care of him?

PEG. What else am I good at? What, Jack? I don't have any sort of … "skill." Take care of my family — that's what I do — I take care of my family. I'm good at it — it's the only thing I've ever been good at — it-is-what-I-do. When you were little, I — you never left the house with so much as a hole in your sock. Your lunches — your … the time I spent in that school. How many ribbons did they give me — certificates — PTA, homeroom mother. If I had a dollar for every cupcake I baked. Your father — when he started the business, I took him his dinner every night down to that lot so he wouldn't eat junk. And I will take care of him now. That-is-my-job. In sickness and health, Jack, sickness and in health. *(Jack says nothing. Sips his drink.)* Are you going to help me or not?

JACK. How are you so sure he's actually going to go through with it? Tomorrow he might —

PEG. I-know-him. Fifty-one years, you get to know a person and — yes — he is going to do this. When he gets that tone in his voice —

JACK. Fifty-one years?

PEG. *(Slightly thrown.)* Yes.

42

JACK. Fifty-_one_.

PEG. You were at the party.

JACK. And it was a year early.

PEG. I have no idea what you're —

JACK. Mom, your wedding license is in with the will and stuff. *(Silence. Peg stares at him a moment, then turns away.)* Mom —

PEG. I don't want to discuss it —

JACK. It's okay —

PEG. It's embarrassing —

JACK. *(Gently.)* It's not a big deal. *(She sighs.)*

PEG. Not nowadays, no. Back then it … in our neighborhood … it was huge.

JACK. And pretty common.

PEG. Doesn't make it right.

JACK. Doesn't make it wrong. *(She avoids his gaze.)*

PEG. It was a different … time. Now, nobody cares. Anything goes … anything … *(Lights begin to shift. Gunner appears on the fringe, moving like a much younger man. Peg looks at the floor. She seems smaller.)* There's no … shame anymore …

GUNNER. Will you stop worry'n. My God, your nails are bit down to nothin' — *(Taking her hand.)* I'm gonna marry you, Margaret Constance. Okay, you hear me? Next Saturday if you want. Whatta you say? *(She just stares at him.)* You wanta nod or somethin'?

PEG. *(A tiny voice.)* Yes. Okay.

GUNNER. Can't ya smile? *(She forces a smile but still looks on the verge of tears. Her expression whaps him in the heart.)* Please don't look that way, Peg. I know this wasn't in the cards but … I wanta marry you. I do. You believe me? *(She nods.)* Have a party down the Knights. Salvy's mom'll make food. Mike's band. We'll dance. I'll dance you like you never been danced before. It'll be great. Best party that street ever saw. *(He puts his hand on her chin and turns her face to his.)* I'll take care of everything, honey. Don't you worry about a thing. I'm in charge. *(He observes her. Finally, barely audible:)*

PEG. What about … college?

GUNNER. Plenty'a time for that, Peg.

PEG. I can't be a teacher with a baby at home.

GUNNER. Sure you can. Not always gonna be a baby, Peg. Down a road. Plenty a time.

PEG. You really think so?

GUNNER. Promise. Onna stacka Bibles. One thing we got is plenty a time. *(She looks at him, believing him, and smiles for real this time.)* And we're gonna have the best baby inna world. A girl. And she'll look just like you. 'Cause if she looks like me, she's gonna be real unpopular. *(Peg laughs. Gunner picks up the ball and runs with it.)* I'm serious, babe. Could you picture a little girl with my mug? She'd be so ugly we'd take her to the zoo and they'd say, "Thanks for bringin' her back." *(Peg laughs again. Gunner basks in it.)* Got ya laughin'. That's more like it, Margaret Constance … gotcha laughin' … you're so beautiful when ya laugh … Grace Kelly, South Philly version … *(Lights fade on Gunner.)*

PEG. Things were very … different … then …

JACK. *(Quietly.)* I'm sure they were.

PEG. Whole different set of … *(She shrugs.)* You got married, you stayed married. Growing up, you remember, not one broken home in our neighborhood —

JACK. "Broken home?" God, Mom —

PEG. Well, that's what we used to say. There were no divorces in our neighborhood when you were little.

JACK. The Greens.

PEG. *(Not mean.)* They were Jewish. *(A beat. They both laugh softly, remembering. Jack rises, stretching.)*

JACK. Ohhhh … my neck feels good.

PEG. Ibuprofen.

JACK. Right. Ibuprofen. Good old … ibuprofen. *(Silence.)*

PEG. We actually thought that … well, that you and Barb — same situation. *(Off his look.)* We … thought she was … I mean, you're barely twenty — you come home and just announce that you're getting married. We didn't say anything but — well, when it was clear it wasn't the same … situation I … figured it out. The rush.

JACK. What?

PEG. You did it to shut him up. *(Jack says nothing.)* Right? You got married to stop all the … chef jokes. The "three dollar bill" jokes.

JACK. Mom —

PEG. You did it to stop the jokes. *(Softening.)* Hurt after a while, don't they? He never sees that. Just … jokes to him. I tried to get him to stop it — I would see your face, but he … thought it was good for you or something. *(She sighs, then looks out at the water.)* So you're not going to help me. Is that it?

JACK. Sabotage his boat? No. Sorry.

PEG. Then what about talking him into the —

JACK. No. He'd be miserable there.

PEG. You don't know —

JACK. I was there, Mom. Made me sick. People in that A-Wing place — if they were dogs, we'd put 'em to sleep. *(Silence.)*

PEG. Okay then. Okay. *(She begins to head in.)* Gunner said he won't do it without my blessing. It'll be a cold day you-know-where before he gets it.

JACK. Do you hate him? *(This stops her.)*

PEG. Of course not.

JACK. He thinks I hate him.

PEG. That's ridiculous. Nobody here hates anybody.

JACK. I hate my son. *(She reacts, then composes.)*

PEG. I'd lay off the whiskey if I were you.

JACK. He's … useless, Mom. He has no friends, he sits in his room — occasionally emerging to microwave a burrito. And I try to talk to him about college — about the future and — and he is so much luckier than me. He wants to waste four years studying video games — fine, I'll pay for it. I'm not gonna … humiliate him — make him feel like he's … *(Restraining.)* I'm not saying he can't do it I'm just saying have a back-up plan — something. Barb and I can't figure it out — where'd we screw up? I'm not throwing him out of the house or anything. I'll support him, I just don't … like him. He embarrasses me. Go figure. *(Peg reacts to the Gunnerism. Jack didn't even notice. Silence.)*

PEG. Sometimes, when you were a baby, I'd get … angry at you. Frustrated. I was a teenager, I had … plans. Things I wanted to do but … now I had a baby and I was scared and — well, eventually I got over it. You don't … hate your son, Jack. And I certainly don't hate your father.

JACK. Sounds like it sometimes. *(Off her look.)* Some of the stuff I've heard you two say to each other. *(This hits Peg. She moves to the doorway, then stops, unsure.)*

PEG. Jack, please — you spend all those years with a person, you run the gauntlet. You love them and … they make you laugh and then turn around and do something cruel and you cry and they frustrate you — and yes, God forbid, they bore you sometimes — but … well, with your father and I — that has never, never been "hate," Jack. It's just … *(Thinks a moment.)* Fifty years … *(Lights fade on Peg and remain on Jack. He lets out a Peg-like sigh as he moves*

45

to the living room. He sits with the glow of the TV reading Philadel-phia *magazine with a highlighter in his hand. Something catches his eye and he highlights it. He does not hear Gunner approach in the background. Gunner looks a little uncomfortable.)*

GUNNER. Hey.

JACK. Hey.

GUNNER. What do you say to an Italian in a three-piece suit? *(Before Jack can react.)* "Will the defendant please rise?" How does an Italian get into an honest business?

JACK. No idea.

GUNNER. Through the skylight. *(He pauses.)* Damn, had one more. Forgot it. *(Gunner laughs, then sits, still uncomfortable.)* You hungry?

JACK. Still full from dinner.

GUNNER. You ate that crap?

JACK. *(Surprised.)* Yeah.

GUNNER. They're bein' real pricks 'bout what ya can bring in here but I could smuggle in a sausage and pepper if you want. *(Jack sits up. What's going on?)* Have to wolf it down 'fore they smell it though. That one nurse looks like a linebacker — I ain't messin' with her.

JACK. *(Carefully.)* I'm fine.

GUNNER. They gotta clock on me. Only allowed like five min-utes, the bastards. *(Silence.)* So ... what'd they say? When ya gettin' out? *(Jack decides to play along.)*

JACK. Don't know.

GUNNER. Least ya can talk this week. Took that tube outta your throat — thank God. *(Silence.)* So ... you need anything?

JACK. No. *(Gunner paces.)*

GUNNER. Place always gimme the creeps. Only in here once. Three nights and that was plenty. And you hired the dumb bastard put me in here.

JACK. I did?

GUNNER. He was Italian, Salvy. You hired all the Italians. Dropped the palette on my arm — hadda put a pin in it. Christ, thirty years ago — least. You don't remember this?

JACK. *(Lying.)* No.

GUNNER. Put me in here. Nothin' serious, ya know, but ... I wake up — and there's Jack standin' there. I told him not to come. He's in college — six hours away — seven with traffic, it was a

Tuesday night and — he just wanted to … ya know … see how I was, I guess. Saw I was fine — talked a couple minutes — turned around, drove back ta school. *(A beat.)* I remember thinkin' — after he left — whatta ya know: Maybe … the kid doesn't hate me. 'Cause I figured … ya know, we were buttin' heads back then —

JACK. He didn't hate you.

GUNNER. Who knows with kids. Kids and women. You could take apart an engine, blindfold me, and I'll put it back together. Kids and women — no clue. What the hell'd I know about bein' a father … *(Switching gears.)* All Peg's fault, ya know. That whole chef thing. Teachin' him that stuff. Rainy days — when he was little — come home and they're baking for Christ's sake. Chef. Jesus. What the hell kinda job is that? Know how many restaurants go outta business the first year?

JACK. *(On reflex.)* Thirty-eight percent.

GUNNER. Exactly. Deck's stacked against ya from the startin' gate. Restaurant … it was for his own good. *(Quietly.)* I said some things to him … Jesus … Whatta they call that in golf? Ya know, when ya screw up and they give ya another chance? *(He thinks a moment.)*

JACK. A mulligan.

GUNNER. Right. Figures they name a mistake after an Irish guy. *(He looks tired all of a sudden and sits.)* Boy, wouldn't that be great if every time ya screwed up big time in life … every time ya lost your temper or did somethin' stupid they'd let ya … ya know … do it over … *(Silence.)* Every time I come in this place, I thinka that Tuesday. Him just walkin' in. The things I said to that kid and there he is. "How ya feelin', Dad?" Long drive just ta check on me. Six hours. Seven with traffic. *(Gunner just sits there. He looks over at Jack, confused for a moment, then rises wearily.)* Better get outta here 'fore Dick Butkus shows me the door. You need anything, Salvy?

JACK. No. *(Gunner just stands there, as if torn about leaving.)*

GUNNER. Come on, put some clothes on. Take ya down The Shamrock for a beer. I talked to Patrick. They'll let Italians in today only. Special dispensation.

JACK. No thanks. *(Silence.)*

GUNNER. Don't know how you stand it, Salvy. I'd put a gun in my mouth. *(He pats Jack on the arm.)* Okay, so … I'll, uhh — see ya tomorrow.

JACK. Okay. *(Gunner starts to wander out, then stops.)*

GUNNER. I got it, I got it! What's different 'bout an Italian

Christmas?

JACK. I give up. *(Lights begin to fade on Jack. In the darkness he will stretch out on the couch.)*

GUNNER. Ya got one Mary, one Jesus, and three wiseguys. *(Lights begin to fade on Gunner.)* Ya look a lot better, Salvy. *(Lights fade out on Gunner and rise on Peg. Morning. She has on her coat, purse slung over her shoulder. A woman on a mission. She sees Jack rising from the couch.)*

PEG. You slept down here?

JACK. Sort of. *(She picks up the* Philadelphia *magazine up off the floor as we hear Gunner whistling offstage.)*

PEG. He's whistling again!

JACK. I know.

PEG. He's doing it on purpose! He knows it'll drive me crazy!

JACK. He's just … happy.

PEG. How can he be happy?!

JACK. Relieved, okay? I don't know. He feels relieved. *(Whatever Jack has highlighted in the magazine catches her eye.)* Look, Mom, Dad came down last night — you were asleep — and he … he was really confused. He started talking to me like I was —

PEG. What is this? *(She holds out the magazine.)*

JACK. That's … that's nothing, Mom.

PEG. Nine hundred thousand?

JACK. Mom, it's nothing. A joke —

PEG. You'll have enough left over for renovations —

JACK. Mom —

PEG. Or advertising or — I don't know — works out great for you, doesn't it?

JACK. *(Angry.)* I was not in on this — okay!

PEG. You expect me to believe that? When I find — *(She picks up the magazine.)* This! I mean is this some kind of coincidence? I find that very hard to believe — *(Gunner enters.)*

GUNNER. Keep it down. Tryin' ta watch *Cops.* *(To Jack.)* They're in Georgia. Nobody owns a shirt, swear ta God. *(He starts to exit.)*

PEG. Want to know what your son's doing with the money?

GUNNER. None'a my business. *(She hands him the magazine.)* He bought a magazine. *(To Jack.)* Couldn't ya get a *Playboy* or somethin'?

PEG. Will you look at it?

GUNNER. I don't have my glasses. *(She hands it to Jack.)*

PEG. Read it.

JACK. Mom, gimme a break here —

GUNNER. Read it and shut 'er up, Jack. There's a hooker sting next. They're hilarious. *(Jack takes the magazine.)*

JACK. "Beautiful Bucks County. Sixty minutes from Philadelphia. Twelve-room bed and breakfast on three acres overlooking the Delaware River —"

GUNNER. That's a great idea! Peg — gimme your — *(He can't think of the word.)* Your ... *(Peg takes her glasses off her head and hands them to him.)* This it?

JACK. Yeah.

GUNNER. And this is the view? The river here?

JACK. I guess —

GUNNER. Peg, you see this? Gorgeous. How much they want?

JACK. Dad, I'm not planning on —

GUNNER. You let Dave handle this. He'll talk 'em down. Can you make money with just twelve rooms?

JACK. I don't know. I was just —

PEG. Stop it! Stop it — both of you — you expect me to believe this little ... act you're putting on? How stupid do you think I am?

GUNNER. This a trick question?

JACK. Dad —

PEG. You announce he's getting a million dollars and — bingo! — a few hours later he just happens to have it spent! That money's burnin' a hole in your pocket — *(Jack pulls out his cell phone and shoves it into Peg's hands.)*

JACK. Call Barb! Call her! Right now! Tell her to go down the basement and check those boxes on the top shelf. Know what I got down there? *(Waves the magazine.)* Boxes fulla these! And those real estate fliers you get outside the grocery store. All of 'em — all of 'em, Mom! — have properties or ... or ... "business opportunities" highlighted or circled or — ten, twelve years' worth! I didn't just start this yesterday 'cause I thought I was getting his money. It's what I do for fun, okay? It's pathetic but it's what I do. Sometimes I go and actually look at them. Open house once in a while. Walk around inside. Think ... think about ... just ... doing ... *something*, besides ... *(He restrains, taking a deep breath.)* You want to believe me, Mom? Or you want to call Barb? *(Peg says nothing. Gunner looks embarrassed to have heard this.)*

PEG. I don't ... need to call Barb. I'm sorry. *(Moving away.)* I have to ... I have errands ... *(She exits. Jack lets out a Peg-like sigh and looks over to Gunner.)*

JACK. I did not come down here expecting any ... money.

GUNNER. I know. *(Silence.)* You wanta watch *Cops?* They got a hooker sting comin' up.

JACK. No thanks. *(Gunner starts out, then stops.)*

GUNNER. Jack? Know what I think? *(Jack turns to him.)* I think you oughta buy the goddamned place.

JACK. Dad ...

GUNNER. I'm serious. Listen to what I'm sayin' here. What the hell you got to lose. Do it!

JACK. I don't know, Dad. Thirty-eight percent of restaurants go under the first year. *(Jack smiles. It's a joke. But it falls flat. Gunner stands a moment, suddenly looking very sad. He starts to say something — stops. Finally:)*

GUNNER. Jesus, don't ... say ... stuff like that ...

JACK. Just kiddin', Dad —

GUNNER. Well, don't — okay? Don't ... *(His voice trails off.)* Look, I uhh ... I'm ... sorry ... ya know, I'm just ... *(Lights begin to fade on Gunner as Jack moves to the beach.)* You take that money, you hear me. And you do whatever the hell you want with it. Maybe it'll ... make up for some stuff. *(Lights fade on Gunner and rise on the beach. Near dusk. Jack picks up a stone and — carefully due to his neck — skips it. His face brightens; it looks good. He silently counts ... to two.)*

JACK. Shit. *(He reaches down for another stone as Peg comes around the house from the front. She has her purse over her shoulder and her cell to her ear.)* Hey.

PEG. *(Whispering.)* I'm on hold. Where's Gunner?

JACK. Inside. Where've you been all day? You just took off.

PEG. I have been everywhere — *(Into phone.)* Yes, hello — my name is Peg Concannon and —

GUNNER. *(Offstage.)* This was the best damn sandwich I ever — where are ya? *(Peg scurries back around the house.)*

PEG. Don't tell him I'm home. *(Jack silently reacts as she exits. Again, he's the keeper of secrets.)*

JACK. Out here. *(Gunner steps out finishing the last piece of his sandwich. He wears a T-shirt under a flannel shirt — and boxer shorts.)*

GUNNER. What kinda mayonnaise was that?

JACK. Homemade. *(He sees Gunner.)* Dad —

GUNNER. You made that?

JACK. Not hard. Dad, where's your —

GUNNER. Beats the hell outta Miracle Whip, I can tell you that. *(Gunner sits as if everything is perfectly normal.)* Eatin' like a pig today. Probably put on five pounds. Go figure. Help me sink faster. *(He laughs, no reaction from Jack.)* That's the one good thing about dyin': You can do whatever the hell you want. *(Modeling.)* No sunscreen. Screw that. I got half a mind to go into town and pick up a carton of Pall Malls. *(Laughs, then glances around.)* Mom's not here, is she? She's not findin' this funny at all.

JACK. Aren't you cold, Dad?

GUNNER. Nahh. Beautiful day. Where'd she go?

JACK. No idea.

GUNNER. Sun's goin' down. Better get home soon.

JACK. Dad, where's your pants?

GUNNER. Whatta ya talkin' about?

JACK. Your pants. *(Gunner looks confused, then glances down. He realizes … and his body seems to slump. He rises, disgusted.)*

GUNNER. Christ …

JACK. You had 'em on when I made you the sandwich.

GUNNER. I know, I know. *(He exits into the house.)*

JACK. Why'd you take 'em off?

GUNNER. *(Offstage. Sharp.)* I don't know, Jack. Okay? I don't know. *(Silence.)* Don't tell your mother. *(Jack rolls his eyes in silence.)*

JACK. Need any help?

GUNNER. *(Offstage.)* I can still work my pants!

JACK. Okay, okay … *(Jack retreats, staring off at the water. Gunner reenters still putting on his pants, then notices Jack.)*

GUNNER. You okay?

JACK. Yeah.

GUNNER. Don't look it —

JACK. How do you want me to look, Dad?

GUNNER. Just not like that.

JACK. Well I'm not "okay" — I'm far from it. Jesus … I — I don't know what I'm supposed to … do here, Dad, okay. *(He reaches out, holding onto Jack's arm. The gesture throws Jack for a moment.)*

GUNNER. Jack, this whole … thing … *(Points to his head.)* I can't think of anybody I hate enough to wish this on 'em. Not even your Uncle Mike. Heart attack — gettin' hit by a bus — that I could deal with. Bang — all over. My old man — right in his sleep.

Like that. And I remember everybody walkin' around — "Oh, so tragic." I'm six years old, right, but I'm thinkin', "Tragic for who?" Not him, that's for sure. He was lucky. *(Jack says nothing at first, trying to process all this.)*

JACK. I could stop you, ya know.

GUNNER. Today, yeah — maybe. *(Smiling.)* You gonna? *(Jack says nothing, then avoids.)*

JACK. Okay, what if this is all a moot point? What if she doesn't … write off on it. Give her blessing — whatever.

GUNNER. She has to. She promised. Saint Paddy's Day.

JACK. Promised what?

GUNNER. She knows. *(Peg enters. They both turn to her. She stands a second, then takes out the brochure. The second Gunner sees it:)* Peg, please — *(She tears it in half.)*

PEG. I took us off the waiting list.

JACK. Didn't think you were on the waiting list, Mom. *(She avoids his gaze, embarrassed at her earlier fib.)*

PEG. Well … we were. *(She tosses the pieces and moves to them.)* I've been in town, talking to people. And … and … we can stay here.

GUNNER. Peg —

PEG. Right here. In your own house. With the water and fishing and — when the time comes we bring in a visiting nurse.

GUNNER. You know how much that'll cost?

PEG. *(Plowing on.)* And down the road they have hospice and they can —

GUNNER. Just stop right there, will ya —

PEG. You win, okay, Gunner. You win. As always. You win.

GUNNER. Great. So I can wet my bed at home. *(He heads into the house.)*

PEG. Damnit! God … damnit! What do you want me to do?! What?

GUNNER. *(Quietly.)* Already told ya. *(She takes a deep breath, calming.)*

PEG. Okay … okay. *(A beat.)* I've been doing a lot of thinking and … Gunner, believe me, I'm trying to … understand … what it is you're … *(Her sigh.)* Okay, I was on the computer half the night and we can do a thing called a "living will." It'll say not to … "resuscitate" or — or if you're … hooked up to a machine we can —

GUNNER. Oh, that's swell, Peg. Lay there a couple years hopin' for a power failure.

PEG. You don't know that. The doctors —

GUNNER. Don't start with those bastards. Why'd you go to mass all those years, Peg? Wanta see God? Make an appointment and sit in the damn waiting room for three hours because that's what those bastards think they are.

PEG. It's their job — what do you want them to do?

GUNNER. Get realistic. You bet a horse that loses every time ya stop bettin' that horse. When you gotta feed somebody Jello inna tube, it's time to give up. Why is that so tough? *(As he heads inside.)* We're so goddamned smart nowadays, we're too dumb to know when it's over. *(He exits into the house. Peg stands, stunned, then turns to Jack.)*

PEG. What'm I supposed to do, Jack? For God's sake, I'm trying —

JACK. I know —

PEG. What am I — he doesn't want to go into a — fine — he doesn't have to —

JACK. I know, Mom —

PEG. I'm making adjustments! Concessions — my whole life, my whole life I've been the one to — but no — no — not ... good enough — not good enough — never good enough —

JACK. He just —

PEG. What? Just what?

JACK. He's ... made up his mind.

PEG. And the rest of us all just go along with it. Gunner has spoken and we all just —

JACK. It's none of our business — *(Jack reaches out as if trying to comfort her but she pushes his hand away.)*

PEG. It is so my "business." This time tomorrow I'm ... I'm alone. Have you thought about that, huh, have you? That crossed your mind at all — I'm alone! *(She quickly glances up at the house, afraid Gunner may have heard her. Silence. Jack backs away, looking out at the water.)* I don't ... enjoy being the ... bad guy here, Jack. If you ... back me up — talk to him — convince him he doesn't have to go to any —

JACK. No! I'm not gonna make it any rougher on him — I'm not gonna —

PEG. You're willing to let him kill himself for money.

JACK. And you're willing to let him suffer so you'll have some-thing to do! Jesus, Mom, take up bingo! *(She is shocked by this and the minute he says it he regrets it. Silence.)* Mom, the whole thing with the money — he, I don't know, he ... just wants to ... try and

53

make up for some things ... *(He shrugs.)* He tried. He tried, he did, he just ... made some mistakes. We all do. Christ, Tim — I mean, some of the things I've said to that kid ... God, I wish I could ... *(Silence.)* He ... wants to be forgiven, I guess. Doesn't want to leave thinkin' we hate him. Come on, Mom. Please, just — *(But that's as far as he gets. We hear whistling offstage as Gunner approaches.)*

PEG. *(Re: whistling.)* There he goes again. *(Gunner enters. He carries the bottle of whiskey. Silence as he comes down to the beach.)* Gunner, don't.

GUNNER. Peg —

PEG. Please. You can stay here, I swear. *(Turning to Jack.)* Jack — for God's sake say something.

JACK. *(Simply.)* What? *(Gunner extends his hand. Jack would prefer a hug but that's not Gunner's style. Then he moves tentatively to Peg.)*

GUNNER. Gotta do this, Peg.

PEG. No, you don't.

GUNNER. Yes, I do. Please, Peg, you gotta understand — for the first time in ... who knows? — ever since those damn doctors told me I was ... *(His voice trails off as he looks for the words.)* Look at me. When's the last time ya saw me like this? I-feel-good, Peg. Right now — knowin' I'm not gonna haveta — I feel ... so good. You can't begin to understand how ... scared I've been. When I walked outta that place you wanta put me in. My hands ... they were like this. *(Indicates shaking.)* I was so scared of endin' up there. When you ever see me scared, Peg? But I swear ta God my hands were ... resta my life just ... just ... layin' there ... not knowin' what day it is or ... *(He takes her hand.)* Not knowin' you. *(Forcing a smile.)* If I don't know you ... what's the point? Huh? *(Touching her face.)* What's the point? Please, Peg, make it easy, huh? Please? Tell me it's okay.

PEG. *(Quietly.)* No. *(Gunner reaches out, stroking her hair gently, then kissing her. Peg suddenly clutches onto him. He finally pulls back, looking right at her.)*

GUNNER. Grace Kelly ... *(Gunner smiles, touches her face one more time, then heads towards the dinghy.)* When you change your mind —

PEG. I won't —

GUNNER. You will. I know you, Margaret Constance. I'll circle around till you do. Just wave or somethin', okay?

PEG. Gunner —

GUNNER. Peg, just … wave, okay? Please. *(He brushes his hand gently across her face. She wants to react but doesn't. Gunner exits. Jack sits on the steps. Peg looks off, then turns and starts towards the house.)*
PEG. I've got to start dinner.
JACK. Mom —
PEG. I don't know why he's … making us go through all this. He'll come back. You'll see. He'll finish that bottle and come home and we'll have dinner and — *(They both react to the sound of the boat's motor roaring to life. They stand in silence a moment, looking off at it. The motor fades as the boat pulls away. It will fade in and out as Gunner circles.)*
JACK. He said you promised him something. *(No reaction.)* Did you? Something about Saint Patrick's Day — *(Gunner appears above them. Jack never acknowledges him.)*
PEG. He's said a lot of things lately —
GUNNER. Salvy died tonight, babe. Saint Paddy's Day. That bastard.
JACK. Did you?
GUNNER. Hadda screw up my holiday. Couldn't do it on Columbus Day, nooo …
JACK. Come on —
GUNNER. I was there.
JACK. Did you promise him something, Mom? *(Lights dim on Jack as she turns to Gunner.)*
GUNNER. His heart actually stopped. It stopped, Peg. He was layin' there, no pain — peace! — finally! — looked like he was actually smilin' — and then they bring in some other machine and revived him for ten minutes. The poor guy's fulla cancer, he's screamin' — and they just … I don't get it — they won't let 'em go. What the hell is so tough about that? Just … let 'em go … *(She moves closer to him.)* Never let that happen to me, Peg. Jesus, don't ever … promise me, okay?
PEG. *(Gently.)* How are you so sure that you'll go first?
GUNNER. *(Smiling.)* That's the plan, babe. When I go, you'll be fine. I know that. Hell, ya might be better off. *(Simply.)* But I could never live without you. No way. So promise me, Margaret Constance. They ever put me on some machine, you unplug it. And don't let some damn priest change your mind. Come on … promise.
PEG. Gunner —
GUNNER. Promise.

PEG. Okay. I promise.

GUNNER. Good. *(As the lights fade on him.)* And you better keep it. 'Cause you know what happens to good Catholic girls who break their promises ... *(Lights rise on Jack. In the darkness he has picked up some stones. He skips one. Two bounces. He turns to his mother who is still deep in thought and skips the next one. He nods as he silently counts.)*

JACK. Five. Jesus ... five. Unbelievable. *(He laughs a bit sadly, then turns to Peg once again.)*

PEG. I never hated him, Jack. Never. I've wanted to ... to ... *(She makes a strangling motion.)* On occasion but ... I never hated him. Never ...

JACK. Then let him know. *(She turns to him.)* Just wave, Mom. Make it easy on him. Please. Please. Let 'em go ... *(Peg stands a moment, then turns back to the water. Finally, she raises her hand tentatively and offers a very small wave. Jack manages a smile.)* Come on, Mom — like you mean it. *(Her hand goes to her side for a brief moment. Then she begins to wave. Bigger this time. Although we cannot see it, Gunner has waved back. And blown a kiss. Peg runs to the edge of the water, now waving both arms.)*

PEG. Gunner! It's okay! Can you hear me? It's okay! *(She blows a kiss back to him and continues to wave as the motor fades in the distance. Finally her arms drop to her sides. She looks over at Jack, exhausted. Slowly, she makes her way to the steps. Jack takes her arm but she gently waves him off. He goes ahead. Peg starts to follow, then stops. She does not move for a moment, then finally turns back towards the water for one last look. Geese can be heard in the distance as the lights fade.)*

End of Play

PROPERTY LIST

Fishing rod
Small cooler with bait
Stones
Brochure
Remote
FedEx envelope with papers
Magazine
Olive oil
Cell phone
Bottle of whiskey, glasses
Manila envelope with papers
Ibuprofen, glass of water
Bottle of pills
2 baseball gloves
Flashlight
Highlighter
Purse
Cell phone
Sandwich

SOUND EFFECTS

Beach sounds
Geese
Assisted living facility music
Party sounds
Truck pulling away
Boat motor